"The cure for boredom is curiosity.
There is no cure for curiosity."

Dorothy Parker

Directions for use

To be honest, there aren't any. The prompts come in many forms. In this book you'll find words without explanation and pictures that collide with text. You'll find fragments of photographs, snippets of overheard conversations, questions, instructions and suggestions. You'll find stories in search of endings and characters demanding names. They're all prompts. How you use them is up to you.

The trick is to be bold

If you want to tell a story, don't tell a small story. Tell a whopping great one. Occasionally you'll come across a prompt that asks a question. You know the answer. Well, why wouldn't you? Everything in this book is made up — so every answer and all answers are correct.

So don't fret about finding the "right" prompt or using it in the correct way — just dive in and let your imagination do the rest.

Or just sit and look at the pictures if you wish, some of them are very pretty.

Using prompts as a warm up exercise

If you want to use the prompts as a daily warm up, try this writing exercise. If you lack confidence in your creativity, this will give you a boost. And don't worry that you're not "a writer" — if you can use a pen you can do this exercise.

This is what you do:

Open the book at random and look at the prompt. Read it but don't think too much about it, just let it work on your imagination for a couple of moments. Now grab a pen, a few sheets of blank paper and a timer. Set the timer for ten minutes and start writing. Don't stop until the ten minutes is up — really, don't stop. If you get stuck write about being stuck, if your mind goes blank, write blah, blah, blah until you get started again. Don't pause to read back, don't cross out, don't correct, and don't even think about spelling, punctuation, grammar, handwriting or even making sense. Just keep writing and see what comes. You will surprise and delight yourself. Honest.

Do this every day and watch in amazement as your creative output increases...

Some people have asked if they can use the same prompt
more than once. Absolutely. Prompts can be used over and
over, in a different place, at a new time, in another
mood. Obviously if you start obsessing over a particular
prompt things might get out of hand. But you're a grown-up,
you know when a relationship has become unhealthy. You
decide when it's time to say thank you and move on.

In the end, of course, you'll create your own prompts.
You'll begin to see them everywhere you go. You'll realise
that life is just one huge prompt inviting you to respond
to it. It's what your imagination is for.

Enjoy.

go on then...

An auction house.

Lot number 14: A chair.

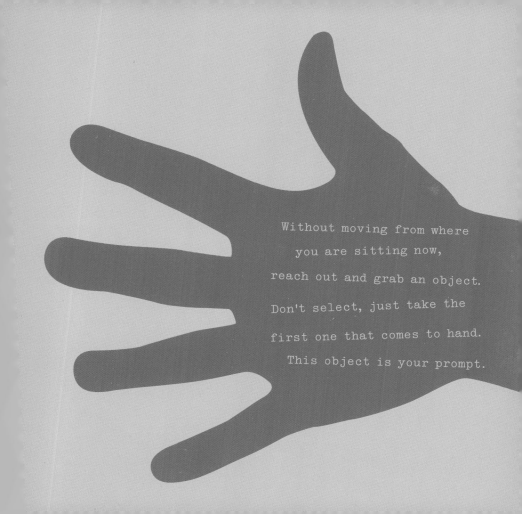

Without moving from where
you are sitting now,
reach out and grab an object.
Don't select, just take the
first one that comes to hand.
This object is your prompt.

Temptation

(be good)

Temptation

(be bad)

When the snow came

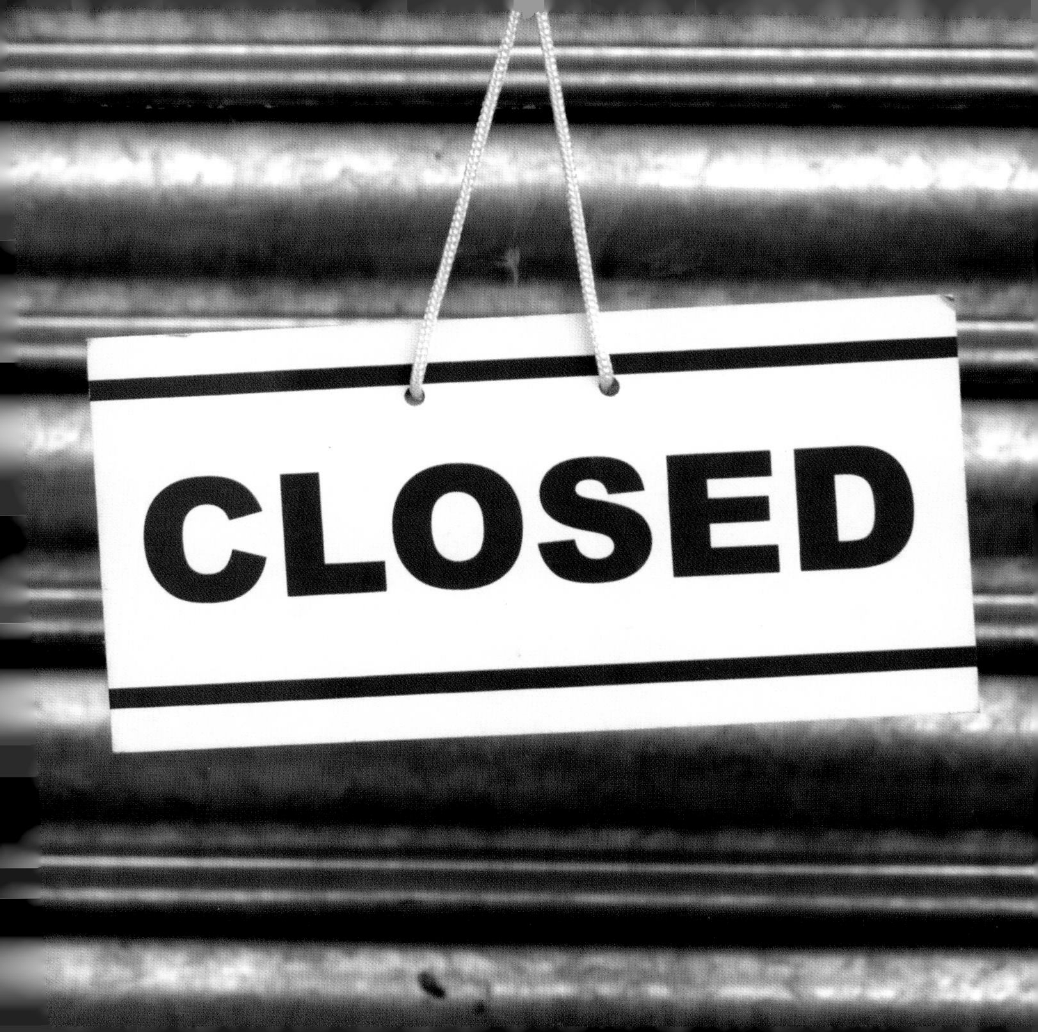
CLOSED

A woman in her 50s sits on the steps of the Albert Memorial in London. She is writing in a diary. Occasionally she stops and laughs.

Read the diary entry.

Find a painting in
a junk shop.

It is of you.

The
opening
scene
of a
road
movie

Describe this colour
without naming it...

A man who always walks in the shade

Very nearly...

(a poem)

1 day

(that's all it took)

Every morning *(what time?)* an elderly man *(name? age?)* walks to a bridge over a motorway *(which motorway? where?)*. He leans on his stick *(it was a present — from whom?)* and watches the cars.

He smiles.

So what's all that about?

On and
on and
on and
on...

te about a character who walks out of a story

RETREAT

ADVANCE

An imagined walk on an autumn evening.

Note down everything you see.

Enjoy your walk.

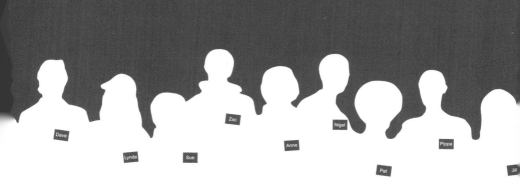

The reunion

Someone is caught in the rain

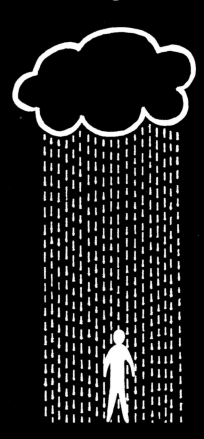

WRITE ABOUT SOMEONE WHO HATES THEIR NAME

AN OFFICE BLOCK AT NIGHT.
WHAT SHAPE IS THE
OFFICE BLOCK? WHAT'S
IT MADE OF? HOW HIGH?
WHAT'S AROUND IT?
A DARK NIGHT?
OR IS THERE A MOON?
WHAT SEASON? DRY,
RAIN, OR MIST? THERE IS
A LIGHT ON AT A WINDOW.
JUST ONE LIGHT,
AT ONE WINDOW.
EXPLAIN

A house in the country.
It's 10pm on a hot
summer's evening.

What happened here
45 minutes ago?

AN OVERHEARD WHISPER

WHERE? WHAT? WHO?

WHAT HAPPENS NEXT?

"Has a letter arrived for me?"

(the beginning of the end)

A ghost story

Meet

someone

who

is

obsessed

with

their

looks

Watching
and waiting

Walk around for a while and look at roofs.

You will see all manner of things:

A woman in a toga with a pigeon on her head. A man in a top
floor window, dancing. Brown, white, black, silver, gold. Brick,
metal, iron, glass. A roof garden (perfect for secret meetings).
Listening equipment (why?). A tree, a flagpole, two stone lions
looking away from each other. A row of candy twist chimneys.
A weather vane in the shape of a fish.

Note down everything you see. Use one (or more)
as a prompt.

Enjoy your walk.

In everyone's life there is one unforgettable pair of shoes

A

glimpse

in

the

mirror

RUN AWAY AND JOIN THE CIRCUS

Look out of the window. The first person who catches your eye, they are carrying something valuable* in their pocket. Describe it.

(*it may only be valuable to them)

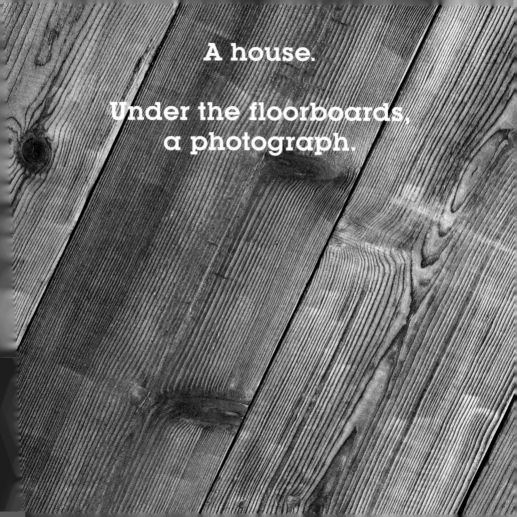

A house.

Under the floorboards,
a photograph.

A love story that involves
a pair of white shoes

Overhear something as
you walk past an open window.

Central Park, New York, on Sunday morning,
a tall man of about 35 is sitting on a bench.
Next to him a is sign:

FREE
ADVICE

The woman sitting opposite is listening
intently. What is the advice?

she had
the kind of
cheekbones
you could cut
bread on

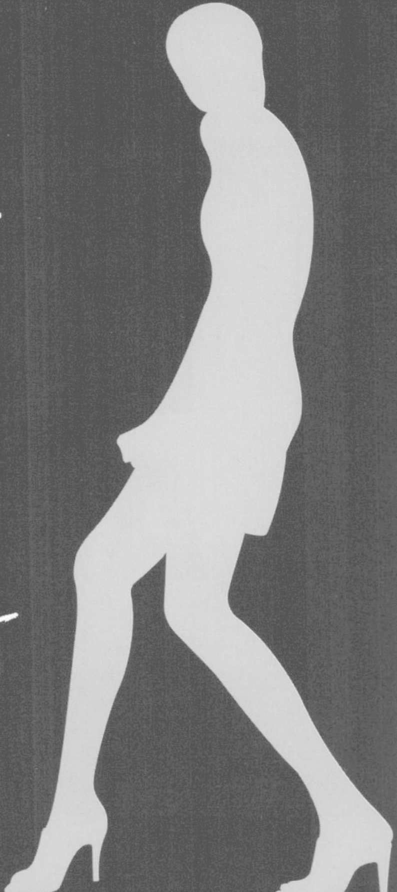

Someone has dropped a knotted handkerchief on the pavement.

A knotted handkerchief is a reminder, a prompt to the memory.

Very few people carry handkerchiefs nowadays.

This person did.

Whatever it was they wanted to remember, it must have been important.

They tied a knot in their handkerchief to remind them — and then they lost it.

Self-portrait early in the morning

Describe a sandcastle

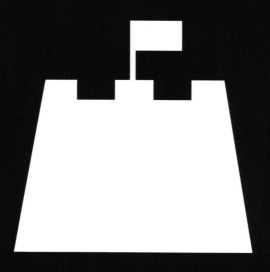

Meet someone very tall
on a park bench

An
act of
concealed
kindness

**Wrong
Person
Wrong
Place
Right
Time**

Write a poem.

Don't worry about
rhyme or metre or
anything technical.

Begin each line with

I remember...

Make it funny.

Write a poem.

Don't worry about
rhyme or metre or
anything technical.

Begin each line with

I don't remember...

Make it funny.

ON THE TUBE, A YOUNG MAN
WITH A SERIOUS FACE IS
STROLLING UP AND DOWN
THE CARRIAGE PLAYING
JOHN LENNON'S 'IMAGINE'
ON A FLUTE (VERY BADLY).

WHAT'S THE STORY?

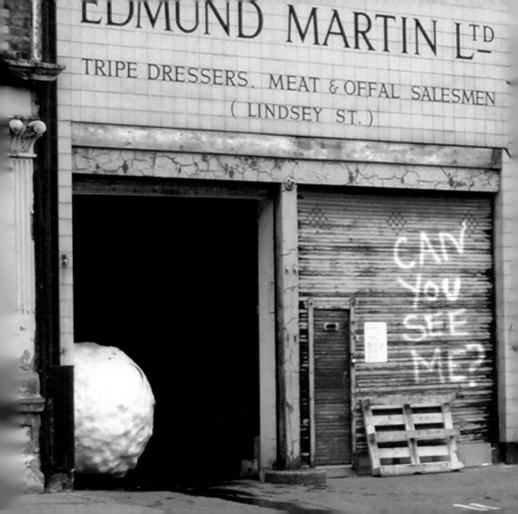

Find an unopened letter at the back of your locker (it's not addressed to you).

Open it.

"Heads or tails?"

"Heads."

What happens next?

Hector Beauclaire has a splendid name. Describe him as he walks through the door.

An August evening when the lights went out

A first date.

You are late,

Very late.

You buy a sofa from an antique shop.
Between the cushions is a pen.

What is the last thing that pen wrote?

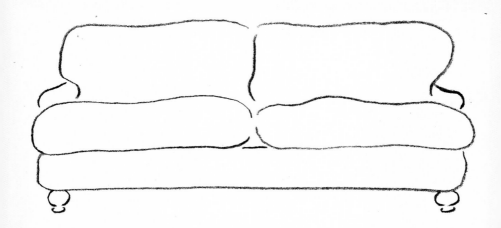

Work

in

progre

A journey

．．．．．．．．．．．．．．．．．．．．．．．．．．．．．．．．．．．．．B

What happens on the way?

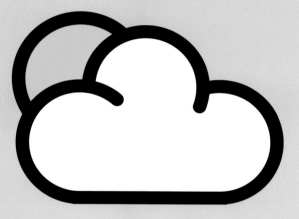

a slight interruption of the light

"I only

met him once,

at 7 o'clock

on an

October

evening.

This is

what

I remember..."

An
incident
that
begins
with
a
missspelt
word

Take a cookery book and open it at random.

The first ingredient listed on the page is your prompt.

The Hat

An acrobat
A woman who sings
A dog trainer
A barrister
A man who writes sci-fi movies
A politician
A game-show host
A wine snob
A woman who walks in the Lake District
A locksmith
A policewoman
A swimming pool attendant
A violinist
A soldier
A script-writer

Choose any 2 and make them fall in love. Or 3 and make it a love triangle ♡△

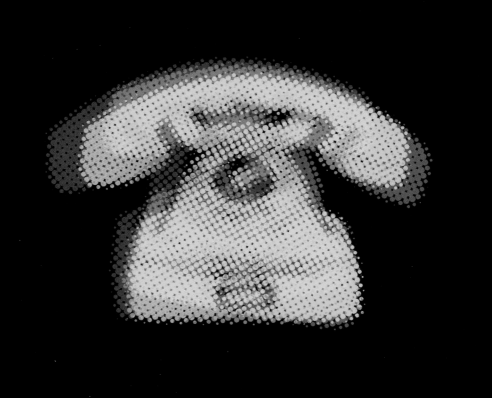

A phone rings at 3 am

A winter night when the lights went out

Three word lines.

tell a story

beginning, middle, end.

Start like this:

'It's a boy'
Over to you.

A woman with a song
stuck in her head

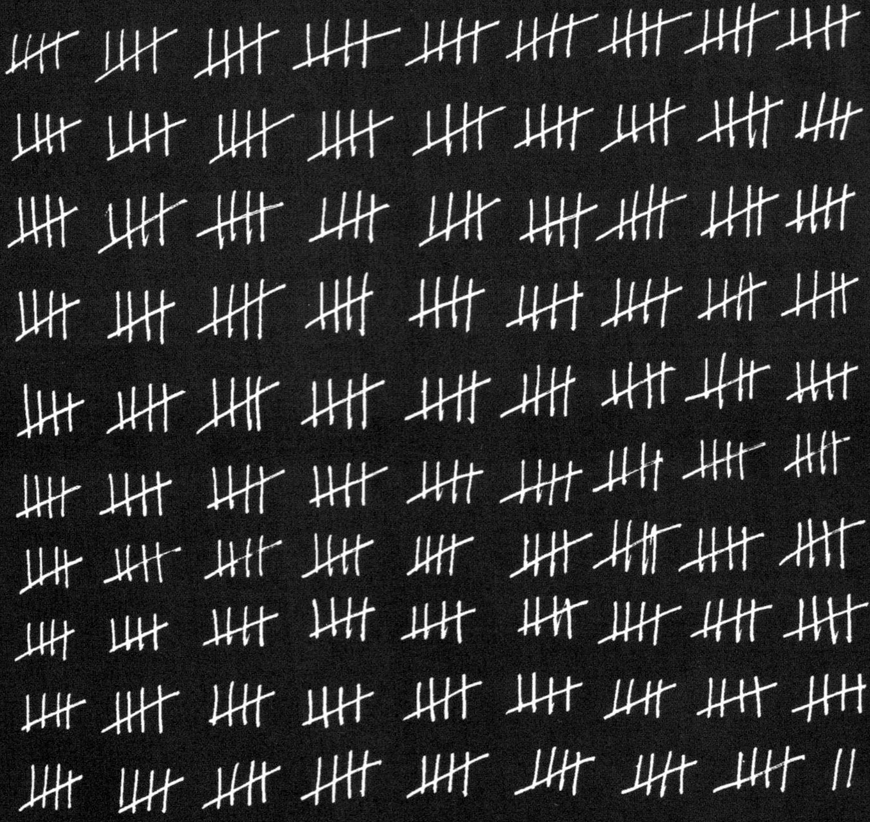

THE
TRICKSTER

Whoops...

Under cover of darkness

An object
is inherited

(there are consequences)

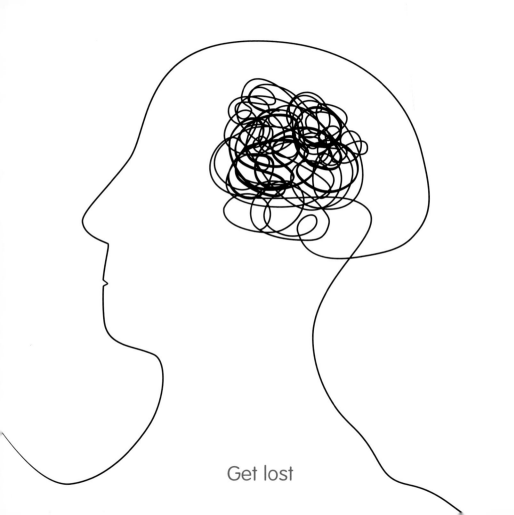

Get lost

When
the
dust
settles.

Write a poem about a flower.

Make it funny.

A restaurant *(what does it look like?)*.

In the corner there is a booth, big enough for two people. A woman is sitting in there on her own, reading a magazine *(which magazine?)*.

One by one a series of people come in, head for the booth and are annoyed *(or dismayed or worried)* to discover that it is taken.

Introduce each of them as they enter and tell us why they so wanted that booth.

A sign in the lobby of a large
office building reads:

Be there when one of them falls.

Every day we are seen on
at least 300 CCTV cameras.

Get caught on one.

Everyone went quiet

THE MIDDLE

The world's most
expensive cup of coffee.

A courier van has broken down.

Just think of all those urgent parcels that won't make their destination.

Choose one and tell its story.

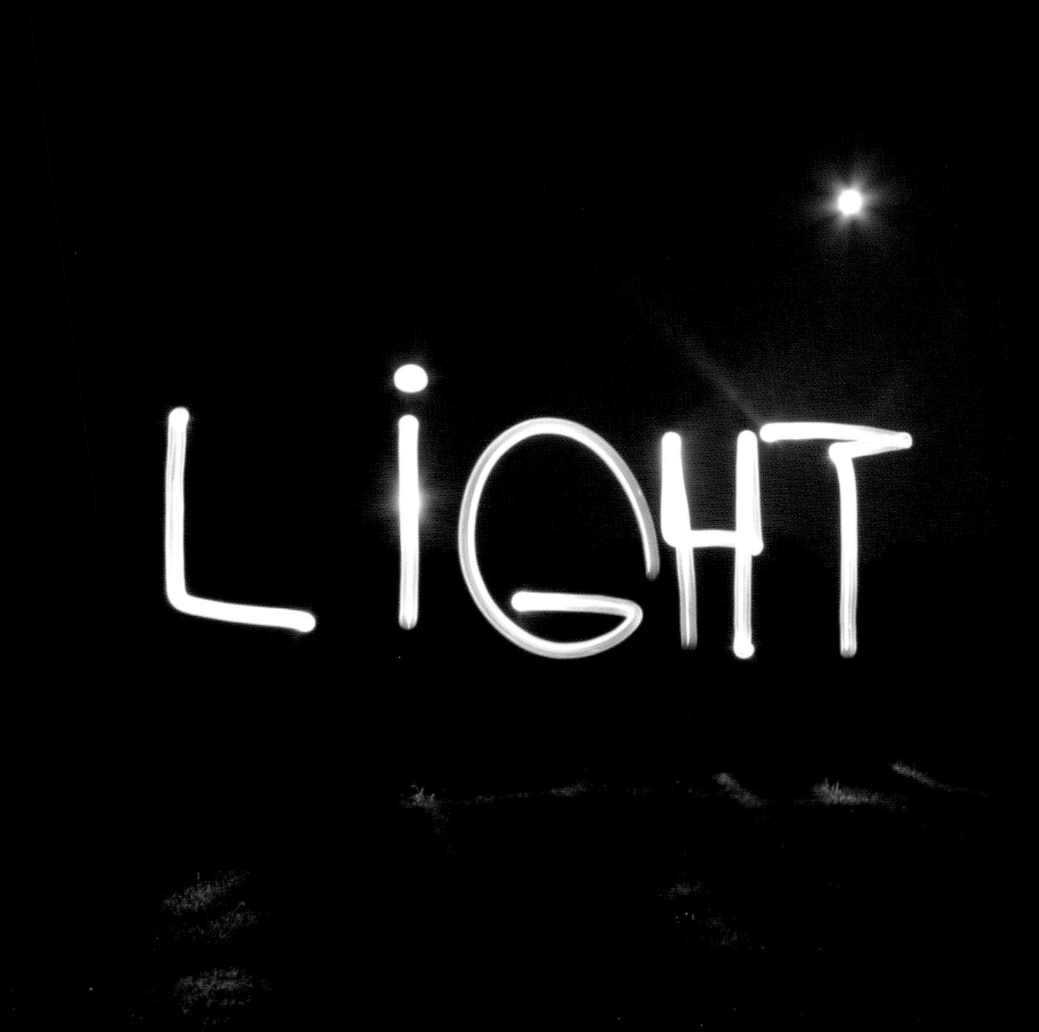
LiGHT

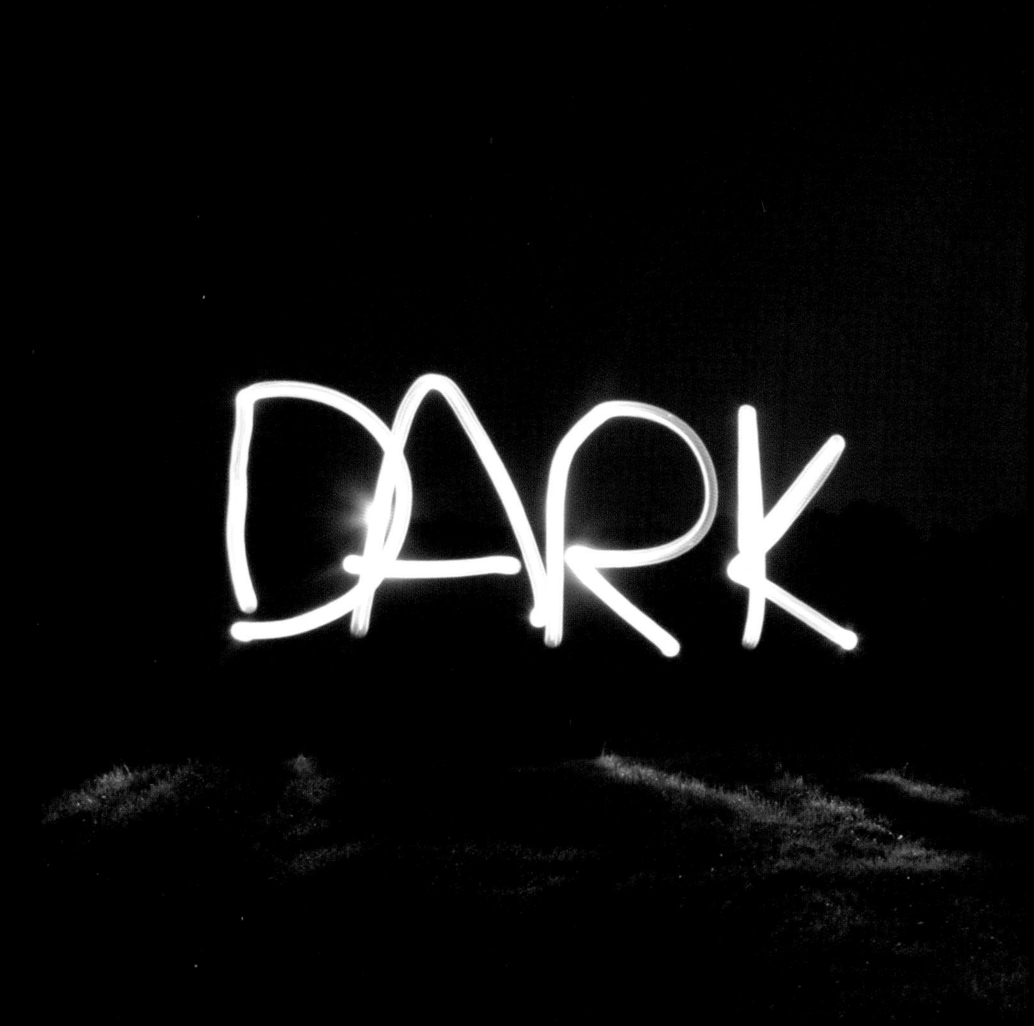
DARK

Wrong Person
Right Place
Wrong Time

10 things she would like to know:

1. _____

2. _____

3. _____

4. _____

5. _____

6. _____

7. _____

8. _____

9. _____

10. _____

Remember the Sound of your school days

The End

So, how did it start?

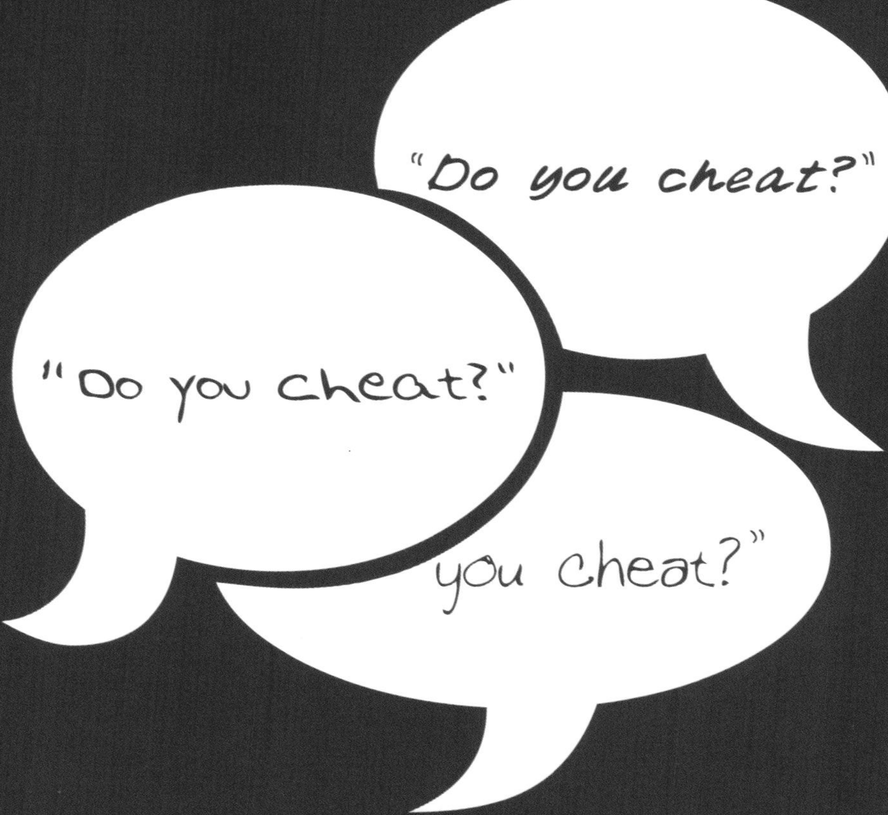

They asked.

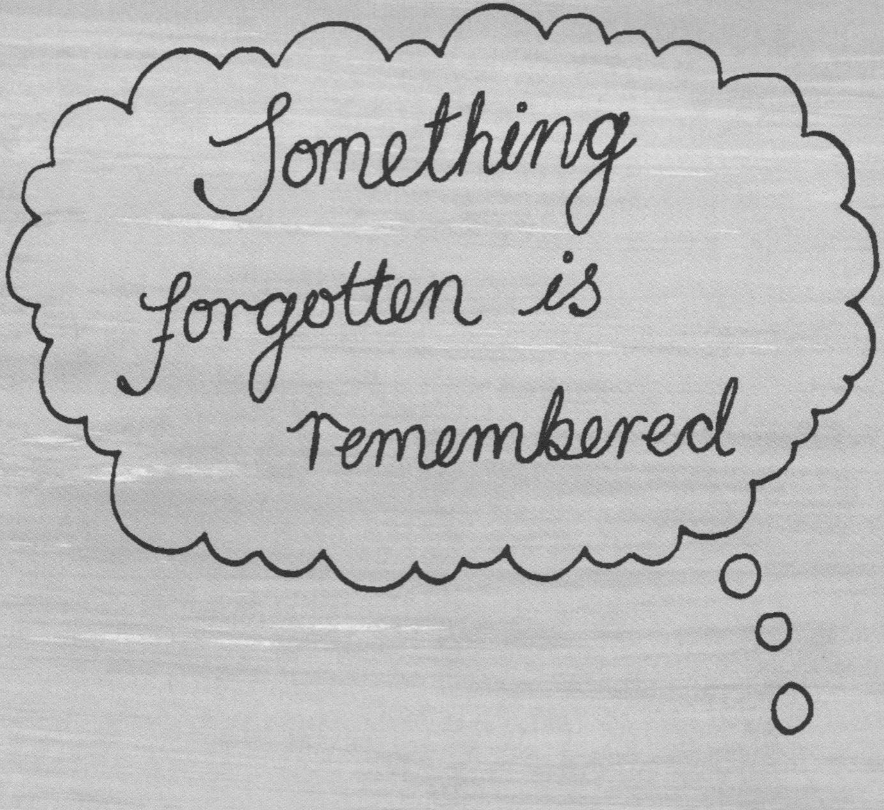
Something forgotten is remembered

ON A BENCH IN A GARDEN:

IN MEMORY OF
MARGARET WHO IN THIS
GARDEN LIVED LIFE TO
THE FULL.

WRITE ABOUT ONE OF
MARGARET'S VISITS TO
THE GARDEN. (MAKE IT
MISCHIEVIOUS, MAD, RUDE
OR ODD – JUST DON'T
MAKE IT SAD.)

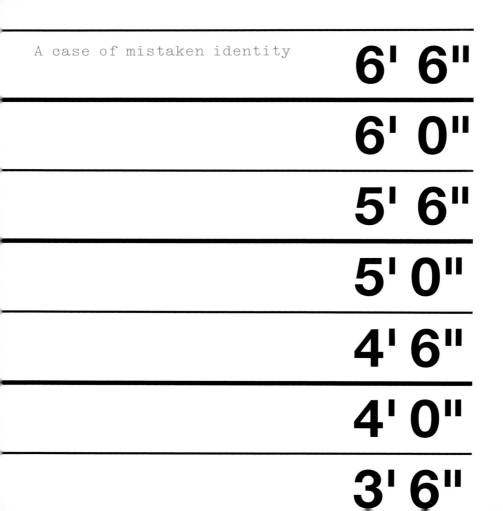

A case of mistaken identity

6' 6"

6' 0"

5' 6"

5' 0"

4' 6"

4' 0"

3' 6"

THE
HISTORY
OF A
TATTOO

Go out and watch hands

Anybody's hands, everybody's hands.

Wait till a hand —
or a pair of hands — catches your eye.

That's your prompt.

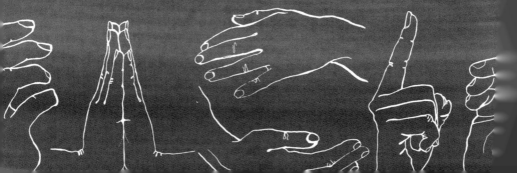

Imagine you are someone's guardian angel.
How do you feel about the person you follow
around all day? Love 'em, loathe 'em or
simply baffled by them?

Now write your diary entry for today.

The Valley of Lost Sounds

(spend a day there)

An argument in a bathroom*
(*the bathroom is important)
"Really?"
"Yes."

A knowing
exchange of glances

LOST

(thank goodness)

FOUND

(unfortunately)

An island called Salerna.

SALERNA

Why would you like to live there?

"Why is the door open?"

Write about something that takes place in one minute

A scene that ends "She kept walking".

A scene that ends "She turned round".

A relationship that comes to an end
when a couple try to name their cat.

THE STORY OF MY LIFE

(IN 100 WORDS)

Name:

Address:

Age:

Gender:

Height:

Weight:

Qualifications:

Languages spoken:

Career to date:

Guilty secret:

Write about the sunrise from the point of view of the sun. It begins...

"Well that was one hell of a night."

HOW TO MOVE A MOUNTAIN

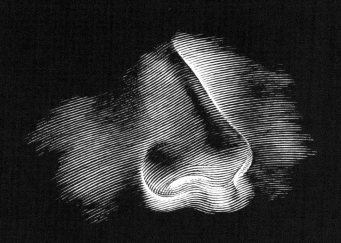

A smell

An incident that starts
when you laugh at an
inopportune moment...

FINAL CALL FOR FLIGHT NO.

BM351

TO AMSTERDAM

TWO PASSENGERS, A MAN AND A WOMAN
DON'T SHOW UP. WHAT'S THE STORY?

Go out and watch the traffic.

Look at the drivers in their cars. Apparently
5% to 15% of all drivers on urban roads are lost.

Choose one lost traveller. Tell the story
of their journey.

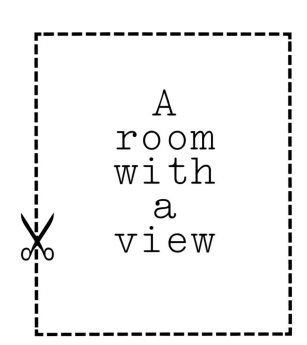

A
room
with
a
view

Describe someone who cries in front of a painting.

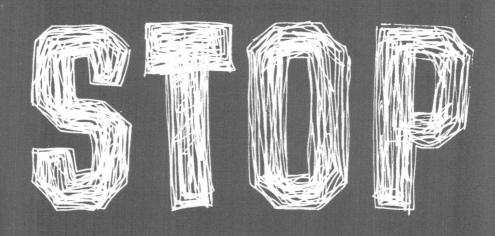

(please)

(he whispered)

The unwanted gift

Two women

Discover you have a
magic power.

"You Dance like a Parisian hostess."

He said.

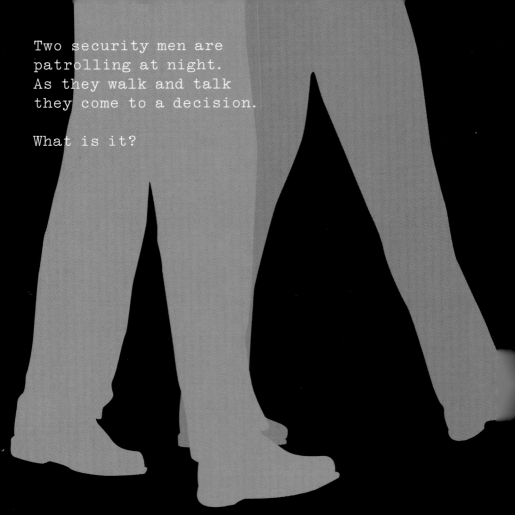

Two security men are
patrolling at night.
As they walk and talk
they come to a decision.

What is it?

a conversation that starts... 'NOT NOW'

THE
BOOK OF
FORGOTTEN
!DEAS

(what's on page 12?)

Waiting.....

Two women...
(friends? family? lovers?)

meet on a bridge
(river? road? railway?)

It's night.
(moon? no moon?)

They whisper.
(what?)

They laugh.
(why?)

They leave...

A pair of red gloves

The Association of Space Explorers is open only
to people who have **walked in space.**

Convince them that you have the right to join.

**A WOMAN
IN A ROOM,
COUNTING.**

Something important (maybe precious, urgent, embarrassing or irreplaceable) is thrown in the trash

The banquet

YOU'RE VERY LATE

A scene that starts with this line.

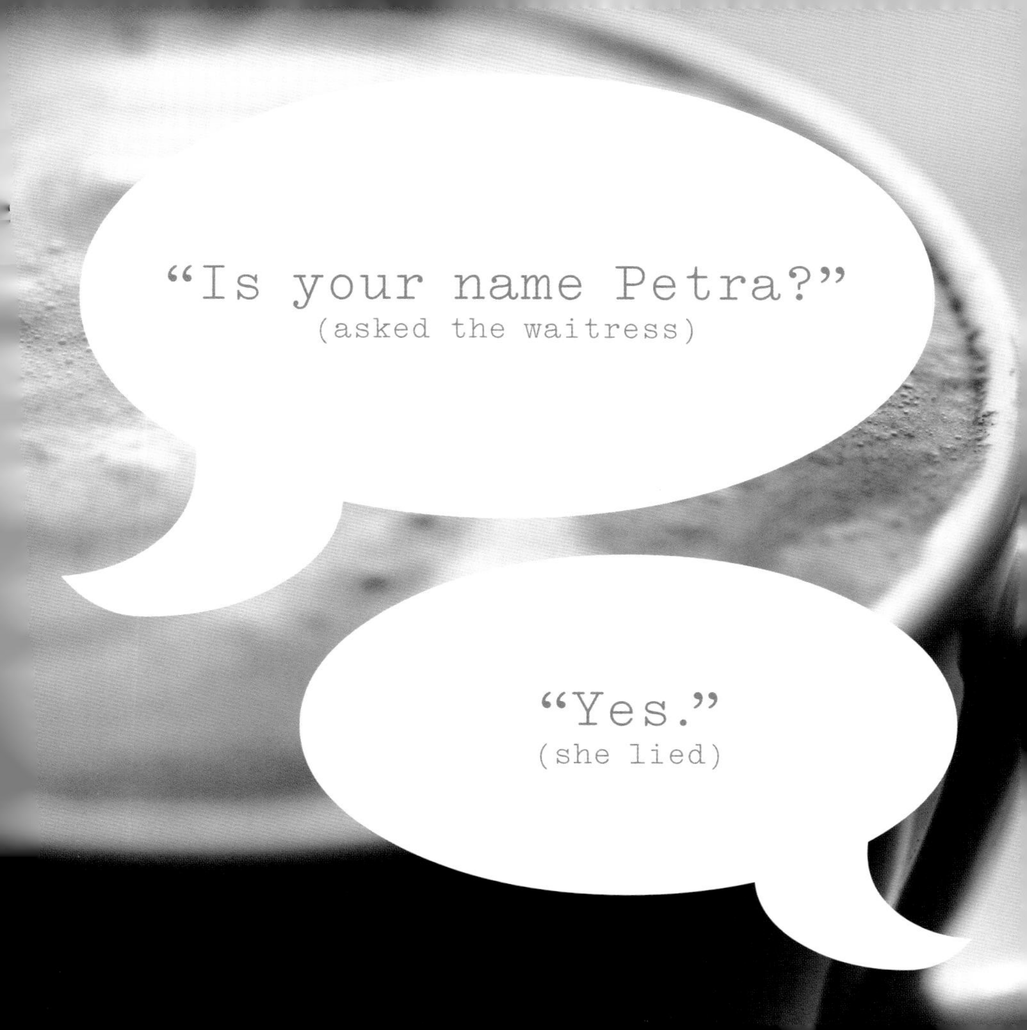
"Is your name Petra?"
(asked the waitress)
"Yes."
(she lied)

HOT

COLD

They hatched the plan in a waiting room

It starts when someone says:

"You could have chosen a more convenient location."

Two men
an overheard phone call
a lost briefcase
and a car chase

A five story house.

Tell them.

After the last guest had left.

Blue

a mood

a wall colour

a nude Picasso

a bruise

a night sky

a himalayan poppy

Sinatra singing Blue Moon

blue movies

bluebell

blue Bayou

true blue

(you choose)

still waiting.....

A bouquet of flowers is delivered
to the wrong address.

(What happens next?)

A secret is revealed

(Accidently? Or deliberately?)

This

gate

hasn't

been

opened

for

years.

After three years she still didn't know his name

The

one

thing

he

would

rescue

from

a

fire

Imagine this:

...YOU ARE

ON A TRAIN

And you really shouldn't be.

You take home the wrong
suitcase from the airport.

What's in it?

(What if) a woman takes a few days holiday in the country.

(What if) she rents a small cottage.

(What if) there's a guest book in the cottage and *(what if)* she finds an entry in the guest book from someone she knows very well. Very, very well. And *(what if)* that person really shouldn't have been there.

Imagine this:

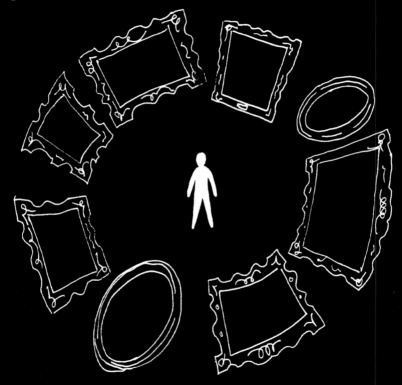

It's night. And you are locked
in an art gallery.

"Did anyone see us?"

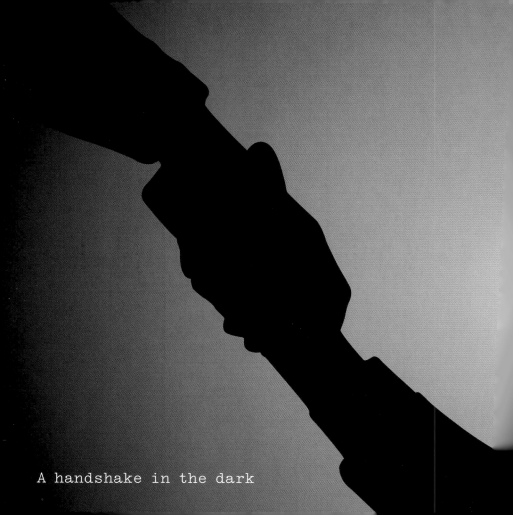

A handshake in the dark

It was a slow day ......●

A cup of coffee is cooling in a garden.

A scene set – well, you decide where it is set. Two old friends meet. No, let's up the stakes and make them old lovers. Write the scene in which they meet. There is one rule. Each sentence starts with the next letter of the alphabet. So, the first line starts with A, the second B and so on through to Z.

Right
Person
Wrong
Place
Wrong
Time

IF ONLY HE HADN'T RETURNED THE BORROWED BOOK.
None of this would ever have happened.

My life as a Mermaid

A small man,

a big problem.

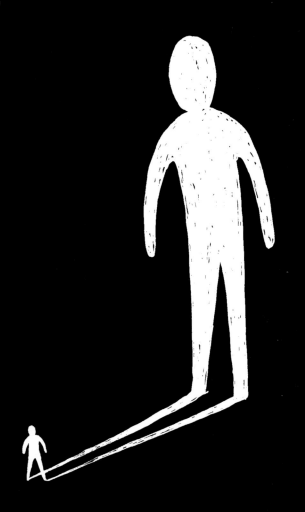

(hurrah)

A PROMISE BROKEN

A PROMISE KEPT

(oh dear)

An abandoned handbag

A LOVE
AFFAIR
THAT BEGINS
AND ENDS IN
A GARDEN
SHED

Walk into a room and fall in love.

what's in the box?

(Be delighted)

LOOK DOWN. DON'T LOOK DOWN. YOU CHOOSE.

What happens next